THE WIZARDRY OF SOCIAL MEDIA MARKETING

CLAMPING DOWN THE CHALLENGES ON SOCIAL MEDIA MARKETING AND DRIVE ENDLESS TRAFFICS TO YOUR MARKETING SPACE.

BY

EMILE MARTIN

TABLE OF CONTENTS

INTRODUCTION

Social networking is a really useful tool for companies. It may boost their brand image, draw in more clients, and foster consumer loyalty. Social media marketing is not simple, however. Despite the impression that the job just entails using a phone all day, it really includes a lot more effort.

We provide social media administration and videography services so you may focus on your strengths while we grow your accounts. We are well-versed in social media and have firsthand experience with all aspects of these sites.

Planning and research are crucial, but you also need to generate and produce material, write captions for it, post it, and interact with viewers. In addition to being a difficult work, there are several more difficulties you could run against. The three primary social media marketing obstacles are discussed here, along with how our company, a social media marketing firm, helps our customers overcome them. I am well-versed in social media marketing and am aware of everything that goes on inside these platforms. We will now look at this in-depth information in the next chapters.

CHAPTER 1: THE CHALLENGE OF TRYING TO STAND OUT AMONGST COMPETITORS_ PRACTICAL STEPS TO TAKE IN STANDING OUT

Trying to stand out from the throng on social media is a problem that many companies encounter. There are firms in every industry, and most of them use social media as a tool to spur development. In light of this, you could find it difficult to draw attention to your excellent goods and services.

It could be really demanding. You are probably blogging about comparable topics after all. Furthermore, it's possible that some of these businesses have a stronger social media following than you.

Even while they may have more likes, comments, and followers than you may think, it's vital to remember that a small, active community is much more significant than these meaningless numbers. Whether a company is large or little, established or just starting started, our goal at Social Directions Agency (SDA) is to position it as an industry leader on social media. We do this by first concentrating on building your social media persona and network. Many brands lose sight of this and develop the bad habit of being fixated on other accounts and their advantages.

We recognize that comparing engagements and follower numbers isn't helpful to anybody and isn't a good way to advance. In order to determine what sets you apart from your rivals, we consider who you are and what you can provide. As soon as we establish a community, we make sure to share things that are relevant to them and give them a sense of worth. The 11.4K community we created for Pods4U's TikTok account serves as an excellent illustration of this in action.

HOW TO STANDOUT AMONGST COMPETITORS

It might be intimidating to stand out from the crowd and understand precisely how to make your company stand out on social media, especially if you're a tiny or newly established company with little funding. Additionally, given that the majority of small and medium-sized companies utilize social media in some capacity to sell their goods and services, it will be difficult for your firm to stand apart from the competitors.

However, you don't have to be entirely original or cutting edge with your social media marketing plan or overall branding techniques; all you need to do is figure out how to differentiate yourself in your particular market or community. These useful pointers can help your small company stand out on social media and attract attention (for the correct reasons).

i) Select Appropriate Social Networks

Take your time and investigate the most effective ways to sell your goods and services on each social media network before launching into the process of establishing a presence on every platform you can think of. Furthermore, you must have a thorough awareness of the social media platforms that your target audience utilizes and get to know them very well.

It makes no sense to attempt to fit a square peg into a round hole; if your target audience isn't active on a certain social media site or your content doesn't fit on it, then it may not be the best place for you to invest your time.

It makes the most sense to start with Facebook, which has over one billion active users every day. Although not every user has the potential to become a customer, Facebook still has value since it encourages the growth of natural connections with your clients. Building connections with new clients requires interaction and involvement. Because of its "workplace" vibe and professional audience seeking to network inside and outside their industries, LinkedIn is another social networking site that many companies find useful.

There are a ton of other alternatives available than Facebook and LinkedIn; in the end, you'll need to do some research and use trial and error to determine which one is ideal for your particular company. YouTube, Pinterest, and Instagram all of which have over 500 million daily users could be very helpful channels for you if you're looking for a platform that allows you to visually represent your goods or services. Remember that there are specialty social networks that may assist you in reaching a particular target market and can be used to set your company apart. There are many alternatives, and that adds to the enjoyment!

ii) Get Ideas From Other People

Yes, there could be a few tiny companies in your field that really shine at social media marketing, and it's a fantastic idea to look up successful companies in your sector to get ideas. However, take care not to restrict yourself or get preoccupied with attempting to carry out their actions perfectly. It's crucial to be genuine and distinctive while using social media! So explore other areas and seek outside of your sector for fresh ideas and motivation.

You may follow a plethora of companies and people on the many social media platforms that are accessible today. A fast Google search for a list of some of the most inspirational social media accounts from all sectors and genres is an excellent place to start.

Additionally, don't be afraid to establish connections with industry influencers on social media. They might be a very useful instrument for advertising your goods and services. In fact, a peer's recommendation influences 92% of customers to make a purchase, according to Digital Intelligence Today. You may have a good chance of differentiating yourself from your rivals and increasing sales if the influencers you target are loyal followers who like your product.

iii) Consult Your Audience for Advice

Take the initiative to engage your followers and target audience. Asking them for their thoughts or recommendations on a specific issue can make them feel appreciated and respected, going beyond just interacting with them on social media. You may start a conversation and encourage engagement among your followers by asking a relevant question about the sector. It's a fantastic tool for getting customer feedback on your goods and services as well.

By doing this, you'll not only be able to communicate to your target audience how much you value them, but also how much you trust them. Since trust is always a two-way street, doing this will help you gain their trust.

iv) Suggest People Who Could Assist Your Followers

Keeping an eye on what your fans are saying on social media is crucial to growing your following and maintaining engagement with them. Do they have any more needs than what you can provide for them? If that's the case, suggest a social media profile that would have useful content for them.

Of course, everyone wants to be the industry expert. Fortunately, there are other objectives to strive for on social media. For instance, it goes without saying that you have connections to other thought leaders in the field who could be more equipped to provide your followers with the information they are seeking for. And that's alright just fine! You show your followers your business knowledge and connections by sharing this kind of useful and pertinent information. By giving them helpful resources even if they weren't created by your business you can further demonstrate to your followers and clients how much they can depend on you.

v) Don't Be Afraid to Be Yourself on Social Media to Stand Out!

Remember that your audience and followers want to know about you and your story if you're at a loss for ideas on how to make your company stand out on social media. They will be much more inclined to relate to you if you are sincere, real, and open. Therefore, don't be hesitant to impart knowledge that uplifts you, has significance for you, or even simply makes you laugh.

While showcasing your skills and being professional are important, you should also be approachable. Incorporating motivational sayings and humorous tales that resonate with your audience and convey the principles of your company will help your followers relate to you more.

vi) Make Use of National Holidays in Your Posts

Every day, week, and month of the year is dedicated to honoring different causes, goods, and occasions in order to spread awareness, encourage activism, or just plain have a little fun. There are dozens of national days, weeks, and months for commemorating almost everything under the sun, such as National Lasagna Day, National Trivia Day, and Breast Cancer Awareness Month.

There are events all year long that you may utilize to promote your industry and/or company on social media; some are clearly more important and serious than others. They might be simply one more entertaining or educational method to spark interest in your goods or services.

vii) Advance the Future by Leveraging the Past

Your audience and following come to you on social media because of your knowledge and your interesting, current information. But sometimes, why not share blogs or images from previous accomplishments and events to give people a better idea of who you are? You may, for instance, publish links to your award-winning posts from your local chamber of commerce, highlight staff highlights, or share pictures from your ribbon-cutting event. Once again, it's simply one more method to show off your humanity, differentiate your company, and build a sense of personal connection with your clients and followers.

viii) Give Visuals Priority

When it comes to posting pictures, keep in mind that 65% of people are visual learners. Share not just behind-the-scenes photos from your company but also personal portraits and images that capture the essence of what you do to allow your followers to identify with your brand. Remember to include educational live videos, infographics, and quote visuals as well.

Visual content in tweets and posts increases engagement significantly, regardless of the medium. ones on Facebook that include photographs, for instance, get 2.3 times more interaction than ones that do not. A picture frequently speaks a thousand words, as they say.

ix) Continue to Be Courteous and Customer-Centric

While it goes without saying that any company should aim to be customer-centric, small companies in particular cannot afford to ignore customer service. Though we've previously covered the value of interaction and humanizing yourself on social media, don't pass up the opportunity to express gratitude to your clients for their patronage. They are more inclined to submit positive customer reviews if they are pleased with your goods or services and you gain their confidence.

Take the time to create a unique thank-you video or graphic that commemorates a specific milestone in addition to verbally expressing your thanks. Clients will appreciate the kindness! Additionally, you can express your gratitude in a more tangible manner by using rewards programs to provide your customers and followers exclusive discounts or freebies.

x) Present Your Knowledge With "How-To" Content

Given the intense rivalry in the market, you may differentiate yourself from the competition by providing your followers with industry knowledge via material that is really helpful to them. Make the most of your experience and skills by producing educational films that uplift viewers, provide a compelling message, and meet their needs. After all, seeing a "how-to" video increases the likelihood that an online shopper would buy a product, according to consumer buying habits.

In summary, understanding when and what to publish on social media is crucial for your company's marketing and branding strategy. However, in order for your social media efforts to be successful, you must always be seeking for new and unique methods to differentiate yourself. Focus on the following crucial activities to get more followers and stand out on social media:

a. Decide which social media platforms are most appropriate for your company.

b. Recognize your target audience and the websites they frequent.

c. Write interesting and captivating stuff for readers to read.

d. Make sure to include captivating images
    to your material, such as infographics,
    films, charts, and enjoyable photos.

e. Don't hesitate to be authentic on social
    media and be loyal to your brand voice.
    That is, after all, the main reason your
    followers exist!

f. Make sure the materials you provide on
    social media are current and relevant.

g. Make sure you consistently post on social
    media, leave comments, and interact with
    your following.

h. Share industry resources, "how-tos," and
    other insightful stuff on a regular basis.

i. When using social media, always be
    genuine, kind, and human.

You'll be well on your way to surpassing the
competition on social media if you're willing to

invest some time in developing your strategy and working to include the advice given above.

PRACTICAL STEPS TO ENGAGING YOUR AUDIENCE ON SOCIAL MEDIA

In order to remain competitive and draw in consumers, your company has to have a strong social media presence these days. It might be difficult to differentiate yourself from rivals, however, if they are vying for attention on the same social media platforms.

Increasing interaction with your fans is essential for success on social media. A plethora of social media tactics and tools have been created to assist companies in connecting with their target audience and cutting through the clutter. We'll go over ways to increase audience interaction, expand your brand, and get more followers on social media.

How to interact with your social media following

You can create social media marketing campaigns that appeal to your target demographic and directly interact with your followers by using these five best practices.

1. Determine the perfect audience and social media channels for you.

Selecting the ideal platforms to concentrate your efforts on is a great method to organize and launch your social media marketing. You may engage with your audience on social media and identify the appropriate channels with the aid of online reputation management services.

For instance, WebiMax, an online reputation management firm, may assess your website and recommend the social media platforms that will work best for your business. Then, it may assist you in developing customized social media campaigns for X (previously Twitter), Facebook,

Instagram, LinkedIn, TikTok, and TikTok, among other sites.

Once your company has determined which social media channels to concentrate on, it is essential to ascertain who your target market is. LeadSift and other social listening tools may be useful. Using parameters you choose, such keywords and regions, LeadSift searches social media discussions for pertinent leads. Finding quality leads using LeadSift may assist you in interacting with well-known people who are more likely to become clients.

2. Produce engaging material for social media. The most effective method for enhancing your social media presence is content. If creating content strategies isn't your strong suit, you may want to use a service like SnapRetail or hire a social media manager.

An internet marketing firm called SnapRetail offers thousands of prewritten social media posts for sites like Facebook, Instagram, Pinterest, and

X. You may alter these posts to suit the requirements of your company. This excellent information may assist your viewers become more interested and engaged.

Here are some other pointers for producing engaging content on social media:

Write headlines that attract readers' attention. You need to use attention-grabbing titles in your articles, advertisements, and content. You want to entice visitors to visit the website and learn more about your company. To do it, adhere to following recommended practices:

- Make use of action words and keywords.

- Make sure that everyone can read what you've written.

- Steer clear of jargon.

- To ensure that your headlines are strong, use tools designed for professionals.

Incorporate pictures into your writing. Text-only material often receives less views than stuff that includes graphics. For instance, statistics from LinkedIn indicates that articles using photographs get 98% more comments. Select vibrant and captivating photographs to add with every post since they encourage interaction.

Include videos in your writing. Across all social media platforms, video is a powerful tool for engagement. When feasible, use video. Instead of sharing a link to your video on another site, submit your films straight to the social media network you use for the best results. You want people watching your movies to stay interested and for them to play automatically.

Advice
Another great strategy for keeping website visitors interested is video. You may increase website visitor retention by including video into your content strategy.

3. Make thoughtful use of hashtags while posting on social media.

Developing and expanding your social media following may be difficult. Nevertheless, by identifying trending hashtags relevant to your sector and target market, programs like HashAtIt may increase your exposure. Using these hashtags might help you become more visible to people and capitalize on trends in your industry.

It should be pertinent to note that In the modern era of social media marketing, hashtags are a crucial component that, when used intelligently and purposefully, may greatly increase audience engagement.

4. Request that visitors share your social media content.

Encouraging consumers to share their experiences is an essential component of social media marketing. Your audience may naturally expand when people talk about your brand and share your content online.

Think about holding live events, such as Facebook Live Q&As, and paying guests who talk about your product or event to entice others to share your postings. Another option is to host competitions on social media to promote sharing. However, before you host a social media contest, make sure you are aware of the legal ramifications.

5. Pay attention and respond.

People used to offer you a 24-hour window in which to answer to a request. It was a long time ago. Everyone in our environment is used to receiving answers right away. It is probable that your social media followers will utilize these channels to ask you questions and notify you of problems. You run the danger of losing them if you don't reply to them promptly.

Listening to and reacting to your audience is essential to engaging them. Additionally, it's a good idea to acknowledge and thank people in public for reposting or like your articles and to reply to any comments from followers, whether good and bad. If you give your followers public recognition, they might become your greatest supporters and brand ambassadors.

HOW SIGNIFICANT IS SOCIAL MEDIA AUDIENCE ENGAGEMENT?

While having a strong social media presence is important, the real measure of your success online is audience engagement. Reposts, follows, likes, and comments on your content can be signs that people are finding your messages meaningful. One of the best forms of advertising has always been word-of-mouth, and in the age of viral content, well-crafted word can travel far and swiftly.

Three reasons why it's so important for audiences to interact on social media:

Engaging an audience increases your reach. Audience engagement on social media can raise the profile of your brand in addition to increasing the number of people who see your social media marketing campaigns. Social media algorithms reward meaningfully engaged content. Your TikTok videos and Instagram photos will probably be seen by even more people the next time around if they generate more interest and buzz.

The reputation of your brand is enhanced by audience engagement. Engaging in direct social media interactions with your audience can enhance the reputation of your brand. This is particularly valid for businesses that use social media platforms like X (Twitter) to handle customer service issues. A large audience will know your company values its customers when they witness requests for customer service being politely handled. Plus, these exchanges often count toward engagement, so improving exposure over time.

Audience involvement increases trust. When a consumer or prospective customer engages with your business via social media, it helps to humanize your brand and establish trust. When you reply immediately, answer questions clearly and honestly, and add a touch of humor or well wishes, you establish the basis for successful connections.

KNOWING AND OUTWITTING YOUR COMPETITORS

14 Simple & Ingenious Ideas to Differentiate Your Company.

Small enterprises often struggle to compete. What makes a consumer pick you out of all the possibilities available to them?

Customers should choose you above the competition for a variety of reasons you're excellent! However, it's up to those clients to discover you, take notice of you, and want to collaborate. That's also where the difficulties are.

You may find yourself scratching your head when so many companies are vying for the same clients by doing the same things. How can you differentiate your company from the competition and win over customers?

How to differentiate your company - local feature

This chapter will go over some of the fundamentals you should know as well as some creative solutions to help your company succeed in a crowded market.
Take hold of the life jacket we're tossing you!

Learn the fundamentals to set your company apart. Despite the fact that they are regarded as fundamentals, very few firms really understand them. And that's what might set your company apart. You may attract new clients with ease if you do the fundamentals flawlessly, or at the very least, superior than your competitors.

1. Begin with an excellent website

Nowadays, a website is a must for each operating company, and the majority of them have one. However, we often come across website errors that drive away clients or prevent companies from being viewed at all.

Here are some fundamental components of an excellent website that may make your company stand out.

Make it mobile first.

In addition to giving your clients who visit your site on mobile devices an outstanding experience, your website should be optimized for mobile devices since Google has begun prioritizing mobile sites in its index above desktop ones. This implies that your website will be less likely to rank in Google for

business-related queries if it is not
mobile-friendly.

Having a mobile-friendly website is one way to
differentiate your organization.

Furthermore, 60% of website visitors came from
mobile devices in the previous year, so you
really can't afford to lose out on this traffic!

Make sure it's simple to use.

Furthermore, you want your website to be
simple for users to access. This means that it
should have a clear, uncluttered design, a
well-organized site structure, and sections
dedicated to each of your main services or
goods, your identity, and your contact
information.

Incorporate calls to action

Whether they choose to purchase from you
immediately, phone, or contact you, you want

your visitors to take the next step and become your customers. Ensure that every page of your website has a means for people to reach you and your contact information. Although it seems simple, many forget it!

Keep it speedy

It's a fact that if a mobile website takes more than three seconds to load, more than half of users will abandon it. You can lose a consumer to your top competition if your website loads slowly.

Are you curious about how your website compares? To find your score, use our free online grader!

2. Take control of your local listings

Because your local listings help you appear in search results as well as map results like Google Maps and Apple Maps, they provide you with an additional online marketing tool.

Handle local listings to distinguish your company from the competition.

This is just another simple tactic, but it will help you differentiate yourself from rivals who could have outdated or inaccurate local listings by making sure your business's information is current and includes your location, phone number, website, and operating hours.

Get the appropriate listings.

Making ensuring your company is on the first page of local listings is important when it comes to maintaining your local listings. For the majority of sectors, Google My Business, Yelp, and Bing Business are the most significant ones. Verify that these websites have a listing for your company. If not, take the following actions to include your company:

➢ Publish your company on Google My Business

➢ Publish your company on Bing Business

➢ Publish your company on Yelp

Verify the accuracy of your information.

so simple, yet how many companies still publish inaccurate or out-of-date information? It's quite a bit.

Make sure that all of your company's information is accurate, particularly your name, address, and phone number (NAP). Maintaining a consistent NAP throughout the internet tells Google that your content is reliable and correct, which might help you rank higher. Additionally, it makes your clients delighted when they locate accurate information about your company on the internet.

Make your listings more effective.

Once your listings have been cleaned up, you may improve them by editing your ratings, adding images and videos, and branding your company. These essential optimizations are missing from a lot of postings, which gives you an additional opportunity to stand out!

3. Make a local SEO investment

The process of optimizing your website and online presence for certain keywords that your target audience is likely to look for is known as SEO, or search engine optimization. Because local SEO is how you might appear in search results, it is essential if you want your company to stand out.

Local SEO encompasses a variety of elements related to your online presence, such as your website's backend, content, and offsite elements like local listings, reviews, and more.

By making an investment in local SEO, you may rank higher in search engines like Google or Bing than nearby rivals that provide comparable goods or services.

4. *Pay attention to reviews*

Customers want to do business with the finest, thus one of the greatest ways to make your company stand out is via reviews. Furthermore, since almost 90% of consumers place equal weight in online reviews as they do in personal recommendations, you won't stand out from the competition if your online evaluations aren't excellent.
Use these pointers to learn the fundamentals of internet reviews:

Keep a close eye on your internet reviews.

Identify the primary review sites where clients are posting comments about your company. These often match your top rankings on Yelp and Google My Business. To keep track of new reviews for your company, either monitor it or set up Google alerts.

Answer each of your evaluations

The way you respond to evaluations is another method your company may make a lasting impression. You may win over prospective consumers as well as unfavorable reviewers by addressing the reviewer's complaint, offering a remedy, and following through on your response.

Positive evaluations should also be replied to!

Obtain fresh evaluations

By accumulating a base of favourable evaluations and keeping your reviews up to date, getting reviews may also help you stand out. Find out here how to get Google reviews.

5. Provide excellent client support

Although it's one of the cornerstones of a successful company, not all companies are experts in customer service.

You already know how crucial it is—more than half of all individuals are prepared to pay extra for excellent customer service.

Provide excellent customer service as a way to differentiate your organization.

You can create a company that really stands out by prioritizing your clients and taking the time to fix their pain points and successfully managing complaints.

Innovative suggestions for differentiating your company
After going over the fundamentals, let's talk about a few less common concepts that you may be overlooking but that may really help your company stand out.

6. Hold discounts on unusual holidays

Yes, you may (and should!) continue to run your typical holiday campaigns during Thanksgiving or Christmas, but if you want to make a big impression, you can also use promotions or specials to mark those lesser-known holidays. We are discussing Ice Cream Month, National Cookie Day, and Get to Know Your Customers Day!

Use a variety of promos to set your firm apart from the competition.

Select a random holiday or holidays to base sales and marketing on. This may make your company stand out from the competition and draw in new clients all year long.

7. Create original advertising concepts.

Why not offer a 57% off discount on your order in the midst of all the BOGO and 50% off promotions? or get a free bag of potatoes with each purchase? (You get the idea; I'm not sure how popular that one would be.)

How to differentiate out in the market: Implement unique campaigns or deals

Conducting unconventional sales or promotions that catch clients' attention in one way or another is one approach to differentiate your company from the competition.

8. Organize competitions on social media often

Organizing frequent social media competitions is another method to set your company apart. In addition to increasing your following and viewership, this may also keep users returning to your social media pages rather than directing them to your rivals. To keep clients engaged, consider holding a contest on a monthly basis or implementing some other regularity.

9. Provide a program for consumer loyalty

What would entice a consumer to select your sandwich business over a rival's if they had to choose between the two? That's one definite method if they were devoted to your company in any manner!

Creating a customer loyalty program may help you differentiate yourself from the competition and establish a stronger bond with your clients.

Cultivate a devoted consumer base

Offering stamp cards to customers as a way to reward them with discounts or freebies when they make a particular number of purchases from you (or spend a certain amount) is an easy way to launch a customer loyalty program.

10. Experiment on social media

Indeed, the majority of companies have a social media presence where they provide news and updates about their company. So why not attempt something different to stand out?

Perhaps you gave one of your staff members access to your Instagram account for the day so they could post stories or reels from their shift.

Alternatively, you may broadcast live on Facebook to promote a recently launched service. Examine what your rivals are doing on social media to determine what isn't being done, then give it a go!

11. Take part in community activities
Your small or local business's connection to the community is one of the main ways it may differentiate itself from the competitors, particularly the large brands.

You may differentiate yourself from the competition and demonstrate your concern for your customers who are also members of your community by becoming involved in your community. This can be done by volunteering, attending local events, or sponsoring local businesses.

12. Emphasize your regional origins

In relation to your neighborhood, did you know that clients prefer to use locally owned businesses? According to one survey, more than half of customers would prefer to purchase from a local company than a national one.

Many companies take their locality for granted. Thus, you may make your company stand out and compete in your community by highlighting your local origins.

13. Craft an engaging brand narrative

All businesses have a narrative to tell, but not all of them are doing so! In addition to making you stand out from the competition, your brand narrative may help you gain the trust and emotional connection of prospective consumers.

Consider the socks firm Bombas. Sock sales are their line of business. Sounds easy enough, doesn't it? However, while perusing their brand narrative, it becomes evident that they donate a pair of socks to a homeless person for each pair they sell.

You become a part of their brand narrative when you make a purchase from them, which may persuade you to do business with them rather than buying a pack at your neighbourhood Walmart.

14. Take the lead as an authority in your field.

You can quickly establish yourself as a thought leader in your sector and someone that clients turn to for authority by making the most of your market knowledge. For instance, if you own a plumbing company, you may make and distribute videos, blog posts, and Q&As about typical plumbing issues.

You distinguish yourself from the other plumbing companies that aren't by teaching your audience in this manner. Additionally, you're gaining the audience's confidence so they will contact you the next time they have a plumbing issue!

Make your company stand out.

It might seem hard to distinguish and attract new clients in a market where there is apparently never-ending competition and a constant influx of new companies. However, you can really make your company stand out and develop a devoted clientele to keep your business growing if you have the correct concepts and a solid marketing strategy in place.

ACKNOWLEDGING CUSTOMERS LOYALTY

Any marketing campaign's main objective is to make an impression, get noticed, and draw prospective clients' attention to you. That's what your rivals are attempting to accomplish as well. It's not hard to start a company; the hard part is remaining in business, since our clients have too many options for where to spend their hard-earned money. So, how precisely can you elevate everything you do, including your product and brand, to a high standard? Here are my top six recommendations to get you started.

1. Outstanding Customer Support

You simply cannot afford to lose consumers due to subpar service in the cutthroat industry of today. Providing outstanding customer service should be the main priority of your business. Roughly 50% of consumers said they would go to a different brand after one negative encounter, according to Zendesk (2020).

You may enhance customer service by learning more about your consumers via online reviews. Even unfavorable evaluations have the potential to boost your company. Listening to your clients, learning what they need or want, and learning what they're telling your friends and family are all important components of providing excellent customer service. Customer retention requires keeping your eye on reviews, both favorable and bad, and reacting to them.

Make sure you spot chances to uplift your business and satisfy your clientele! If review management is not part of your customer service plan, you may be losing business to rivals before they have an opportunity to use your product or service.

2. Distinctive Branding

Within the first ten seconds, people create their initial impressions of a brand. This is the reason having a strong brand is crucial. You have to differentiate yourself from your rivals if you want recognition. Consumers quickly evaluate features like consistency, quality, captivating media, and message when choosing your brand over competitors. Consider Starbucks, the biggest coffee business globally, which has a mermaid in its emblem. What's coffee got to do with mermaids? Nothing. However, it sets their brand apart from rivals.

3. Establish A Powerful Online Identity

97% of customers start their search for local companies online. For this reason, having a good web presence is critical to the success of your business. This entails designing a user-friendly, visually appealing website and developing accounts on social media sites that your target market frequents. You still have work to perform after obtaining these resources. To be visible on all of these platforms and to maintain dialogues and interactions with your fans, you must consistently provide new and insightful material. Additionally, you may establish yourself as the authorities in your field by starting a blog and producing well-written, relevant material. To have a strong online presence, your brand should concentrate on the following areas:

- ❖ Search Engines Optimization
- ❖ Developing a Superb Website
- ❖ Original Social Media Posts, and
- ❖ Intense Participation

4. Assemble an Elite Group

It takes a team to realize the dream. The cohesiveness of your team is critical to the success of your enterprise. A team that can collaborate to accomplish a shared objective is what you need. Because there are open lines of communication and a sense of shared responsibility, your staff are more inclined to work closely together and take the initiative when there is trust. A cohesive team promotes healthy competition, innovation, and increased output.

To be really honest, however, I would advise you to use extreme caution in selecting the members of your team. The general financial performance of your company will eventually increase with a supportive and inspiring work environment.

5. Return the Favor by giving back

Your clients want to know how you're spending your money and giving back to the community.

Businesses that are giving back to the community and trying to improve the globe are becoming more and more popular. As a result, you may differentiate yourself from the competition by consistently giving back to the causes that are dear to your heart. Giving back may take numerous forms, such as giving your time to charity, sponsoring conferences and events, or making monetary donations. When you're involved in the community and the wider world and not simply thinking about yourself and your bottom line, people will notice. Kind and generous acts from your firm will not go ignored.

CHAPTER 2: STAYING ON TOP OF CHANGING SOCIAL MEDIA TRENDS

Keeping up with social media trends is another major social media difficulty that most companies nowadays face. The prevalence of social media trends has increased with the introduction of TikTok. We are discussing shorter-lived trends such as "Running up that Hill" and the "corn song." While certain trends, like ASMR and gratifying videos, have longer lifespans than others, it seems that fast-paced trends are what make businesses really go viral.

Trends may sometimes give companies more worry than enjoyment because of their ability to enable brands to go "viral." While it's fun to film the footage, it might be challenging to post it before the allotted time has elapsed. Not to add, it takes time to keep an eye on social media sites to discover what is popular and appropriate for your company. SDA is a firm believer in the influence of social media trends.

In light of this, we make sure that a large number of our clients are following trends that align with their industry and have the potential to become viral. But we save the brand a great deal of time and worry by eliminating that. Experts in social media make up our team. We really like what we do and "live and breathe social media." As a result, we are able to forecast the duration of trends and constantly know what is popular, giving our customers the greatest chance to see rapid development on social media.

HOW TO STAY ON TOP OF SOCIAL MEDIA MARKETING TRENDS

By Following Relevant Sources That Report on Them

Following the sites that provide frequent updates on social media trends is one of the simplest methods to remain up to date. Industry blogs, podcasts, newsletters, publications, and influencers covering subjects linked to your objectives, audience, and specialty are a few examples of these. You may also curate and arrange your information feeds and get updates by using apps like Feedly, Flipboard, or Pocket. You may learn about the newest platforms, features, algorithms, best practices, and case studies that can guide your social media strategy by following pertinent sites.

USING SOCIAL LISTENING TOOLS

Using social listening tools to monitor and assess the discussions, attitudes, and actions of your target audience and industry is another method to remain abreast of social media developments. You may use social listening tools to find the hashtags, subjects, influencers, and phrases that are trending and creating discussion across various social media platforms. They may also be used to keep an eye on rival activity, consumer reviews, and the reputation of your company. Hootsuite, Sprout Social, Mention, and BuzzSumo are a few of the well-liked social listening apps.

EXPERIMENTING WITH NEW FORMAT

Keeping up with social media trends also entails being open to trying out novel features and formats that will enable you to produce more varied and captivating content. To engage your audience in many ways, you may experiment with live videos, tales, reels, surveys, quizzes, stickers, filters, and audio rooms. Additionally, you may experiment with various content kinds to determine what appeals to your audience, such as user-generated, inspiring, instructional, and amusing material. You may find fresh ways to present your brand's personality, beliefs, and products by trying out different formats.

ANALYZING YOUR PERFORMANCE

Analyzing your performance and drawing conclusions from it is one of the most crucial strategies for staying current with social media trends. Your important metrics, such reach, impressions, clicks, conversions, engagement, and retention, may be measured and assessed with the assistance of analytics tools like Google Analytics, Facebook Insights, Twitter Analytics, or Instagram Insights. Additionally, you may utilize tools like surveys, polls, and A/B testing to get audience input and adjust your content as necessary. You can determine what works and what doesn't for your brand by evaluating your performance and modifying your plan as necessary.

JOINING ONLINE COMMUNITIES

Joining online forums where you can network, educate yourself, and communicate with other social marketers is another way to stay on top of social media trends. You can keep up with the most recent information, advice, and best practices in your area and business by participating in online communities. They may also be used for professional collaboration, questioning, criticism, and inspiration. You may

join many online communities such as
Clubhouse rooms, Slack channels, Reddit
forums, Facebook groups, and LinkedIn groups.

TRACKING TREND

Social Media Trends: What Are They?
Trends are the things that are hot on various
social media platforms at a certain moment. The
term "social media trends" describes the
ever-evolving subjects and behaviors that are
trending on social media.

To put it another way, trends are fleeting
categories of material that draw large audiences
and spread swiftly throughout all of the main
social media networks. They may take many
different forms, such as challenges, memes,
short movies, and debate topics.

Since trends are ever-evolving, it's critical to
keep abreast of current developments in order to

provide content that appeals to your target audience.

Gaining insight into social media trends may assist organizations in staying current with industry developments and in determining the kind of material that will interest their followers.

Furthermore, social media feeds are always changing to reflect the newest trends on the platform. Popular and interesting material is rewarded by algorithms. As a result, trends inevitably attract more attention and spark more engagement than any other kind of material.

This has the effect of snowballing. A trend gains popularity as more people become aware of it, and finally it becomes a viral sensation. You can take advantage of this impact and increase your reach and engagement with the appropriate target demographic by becoming involved in significant social media trends.

The following are the main advantages of a company engaging in social media trends:

Boost brand visibility: Taking advantage of well-liked social media trends is a terrific approach to get more people to notice your brand and your content.

Engage and form a relationship with your followers via a common interest by connecting with your audience through social media trends.

Increase engagement: Because trends elicit such a strong amount of attention from social media users, you will see an additional surge in engagement by participating in them.

Social media trends gain popularity when they are simple to duplicate, include a hilarious or emotive component, and are supported by prominent individuals.

You may start taking action to improve your social media presence and attract the interest of a sizable audience by being aware of these variables.

Let's review a few trends that have gained traction on social media throughout time:

1.The Mannequin Challenge: In 2016, a craze swiftly gained international traction in which participants would abruptly stop acting as music played and the camera circled the whole group.

2. The Bottle Cap Challenge gained popularity in 2019. The objective of the challenge was to unscrew a bottle cap without touching the bottle by utilizing an unconventional physical maneuver like a spin kick.

3. Dance challenges: These include learning a little song-specific choreography and then coming up with your own version of it. Renegade by K Camp and "The Git Up" by Blanco Brown are two well-known dance challenge tracks.

4. Voiceover Dubs: A common TikTok practice that became viral on social media is lip-syncing to audio clips from well-known videos, films, TV series, and even songs. Online users are able to utilize their imaginations and provide meanings to brief segments of songs or sentences from scenes that vary from the original meaning intended by the creators.

5. Reenactment trends are those that include recreating well-known moments from films or television series.

6. Prank films: In these films, people pull innocent practical jokes on their friends and family, generally for laughs.
How to Recognize Trends on Social Media
Social media trends come and go rapidly, so in order for companies to remain relevant and competitive, they must adapt to these changes.

A method of keeping abreast of the most popular social media trends is to keep an eye on the activity and discussions around certain subjects or hashtags. With the use of this data, you may spot patterns, examine the behaviors of those patterns, and eventually determine how to take advantage of the momentum these patterns have.

The two primary channels you need to follow in order to identify the newest social media trends as soon as they emerge are social media sites such as Twitter and TikTok.

Keeping a careful eye on the posts made by influential people in your field is another way to spot trends. You may get more insight into the subjects that appeal to your target audience by keeping a watch on the material they provide.

Last but not the least, you may use resources like Google Trends to learn more about the subjects that are popular over time. This might assist you in predicting certain trends and making appropriate plans so that you can produce and publish content at the exact moment when it becomes viral.

It's essential to keep in mind that trends are subject to change, so keeping an eye on them is necessary to remain current.

PRO TIP: When attempting to follow trends, many businesses make the mistake of timing. It may take a while for them to release a video since several team members have to supervise their social media marketing approach, and by then, the trend they were hoping to follow has already died.

Advice for Brands on How to Take Part in Social Media Trends

Businesses should be careful about the message they are giving and make sure it is consistent with their brand identity when they participate in social media trends.

When participating in the newest social media trends, you should adhere to the following recommended practices:

Recognize the trend: Before putting their own spin on a trend, brands should always be aware of it and determine if it makes sense for them to follow.

Maintain proper time: When striking the iron, make sure the timing is correct and hit it while it is hot. It's usually not a good idea to follow a trend that is already fading since it will simply make your business seem outdated.

Utilize influencer advertising When following a trend, it's excellent to have influencers and micro-influencers on board since they can quickly expand your reach on social media.

Track replies: Keep an eye on your comments to watch how your fans react as your business adopts the newest styles. Take their response as feedback and modify your social media plan as necessary.

Make your own version: If you think the trend is already too crowded, consider making a distinctive version that sets you apart from the others.

Promote material created by users: Encourage your followers to create original material with a personalized hashtag or imaginative suggestion to join in on the trends.

EMBRACING SOCIAL LISTENING

Social listening is basically free, real-time market research, despite seeming like a fancy marketing jargon. Basic listening looks for mentions of your brand, goods, rivals, certain keywords, or anything else you choose to research on social media platforms. More sophisticated systems may assess brand emotion, identify trademarks in photos, and more.

This provides you with an accurate assessment of your company's reputation and the attributes that customers really want in a product. Still, knowledge on its own is insufficient. You must use it in real life.

Throughout the day, keep an ear out for inquiries about your sector or suggestions from others, and feel free to join the discussion by leaving a retweet or remark.

For major strategic tasks like positioning and new product creation, social listening is also quite effective. Ben & Jerry's discovered by monitoring brand mentions that most customers preferred to eat their ice cream inside on a wet day rather than outside in the sun.

CHAPTER 3: CURBING THE CHALLENGES ON LACK OF STRATEGY OR DEFINED GOALS

It may be quite difficult to manage social media accounts without clear objectives and a successful plan in place. Your objectives are guided by your goals, which you may then utilize your strategy to attain. For instance, you may utilize your approach to design articles that would help you reach your aim of creating a devoted community. Naturally, if you are unfamiliar with social media, all of this will be quite challenging for you.

It's critical to grasp the platforms well and be aware of what functions well and poorly. Realize that not everything you do on social media will succeed for your company immediately. A social media marketing firm like SDA will help you accomplish those objectives. We hold extensive interactions with customers throughout the onboarding process to ascertain their goals for social media.

Goals might include things like leads and sales, but they could also be about building community or establishing authority as thought leaders in their particular industries. Our strategist develops a plan to assist in achieving these goals after learning about their aims. They create engaging and strategic content by drawing on their in-depth understanding of the social media environment. We are aware that entrepreneurs are busy people, and social media should never be seen as a side job. To see the benefits, it requires committed attention.

CHAPTER 4: SUPERCHARGED SOCIAL MEDIA MARKETING STRATEGIES THAT WORKS

Are you sick and weary of your social media marketing campaigns not producing the desired outcomes? Have you had trouble gaining momentum and successfully interacting with your target audience? If so, now is the perfect moment to outperform your rivals with your social media marketing approach!

Social media has become into an essential marketing tool for companies of all sizes in today's hyperconnected society. It provides unmatched chances to connect with new clients, build brand recognition, and cultivate enduring partnerships. But it might be difficult to separate out from the crowd given the fierce competition and constantly shifting terrain. That is the situation we have experience with.

Imagine your brand's social media pages growing into a bustling hotbed of engagement where updates constantly garner shares, likes, and comments. Your impact and reach would expand tremendously, resulting in increased sales and conversion rates for your company. The good news is that by putting the tactics and advice in this article into practice, you can make your goal come true.

Are you prepared to reach new heights with your social media marketing now? Explore our in-depth guide to learn the techniques for enhancing your social media marketing plan. Change the way your brand appears online, engage your audience, and get results like never before.

1. Establish a Firm Basis by Defining Your Brand and Identifying Your Audience

2. Establish SMART Objectives for Your Campaign Using Social Media

3. Select the Social Media Sites That Are Best for Your Company

4. Disseminate Storytelling Content

5. Using Influencer Marketing to Increase Your Audience

6. Make Use of Live Streaming, Pictures, and Videos

7. Increase Your Audience Through Paid Social Media Promotion

8. Encourage Discussions to Strengthen Community and Increase Engagement

9. The Function of Contests and User-Generated Content

10. Make use of trends, keywords, and hashtags

11. Analyze Social Media and Modify Your Approach

12. Plan and Schedule Your Content for Social Media

13. Appreciate Input and Guard Your Online Image

14. Make sure your whole marketing plan incorporates your social media marketing strategy.
Are You Prepared to Boost Your Social Media Approach?

1. Establish a Firm Basis by Defining Your Brand and Identifying Your Audience

Improving the performance of social media marketing requires clearly defining a brand and determining the target market. Here's how a company can accomplish these goals:

Describe the main goals and values of the brand:

Give a clear explanation of its goals, core values, and distinguishing characteristics. This makes the message more uniform across social media and other marketing platforms.

Determine the personality of the brand:

Take note of the brand's voice and tone, which should be reflected in all of its communications. This might be casual and conversational or formal and authoritative. A dependable brand character facilitates building rapport with the intended audience.

Establish a visual identity:

Make sure the brand's logo, colour palette, font, and images are all consistent. To guarantee recognition and memorability, include these components into all of your social media material.

Determine who the intended audience is:

Identify the psychographics, behavioural traits, and demographics of your target clientele. This covers characteristics including age, gender, geography, values, and online conduct. Producing relevant and interesting content requires an understanding of the target audience.

Perform market research:

To learn more about the requirements, preferences, and pain points of the target audience, conduct focus groups, interviews, and surveys. Utilizing this data, social media message and content may be adjusted to better connect with the target demographic.

Examine rivals:

Research rivals' social media profiles to determine what functions well and poorly. Determine any holes in their approaches or material that may be used to set your company apart from the competition.

Make audience personas:

Construct thorough personas that reflect the various target audience groupings. These personas may direct the production of customized content, ensuring that it speaks to the unique requirements and interests of each section.

By establishing its brand and determining its target market, a company may develop a targeted and successful social media marketing campaign. This will thus support the delivery of relevant material, encourage interaction, and produce the intended outcomes.

2. Establish SMART Objectives for Your Campaign Using Social Media

For your social media marketing plan to be successful and track your progress, you must set SMART objectives. The words "specific, measurable, achievable, relevant, and time-bound" are abbreviated as "SMART." To create SMART objectives for your social media marketing strategy, follow these steps:

Be Particular and concise:

Clearly state in detail the goals you have for your social media marketing campaigns. Set goals like "increase Instagram followers by 15% in three months" or "boost engagement rate on Facebook by 10% in six weeks" as opposed to nebulous ones like "grow on Instagram."

Measurable:

Make sure you can measure and monitor your objectives. This enables you to track developments and assess if your efforts are paying off. Key performance indicators (KPIs) including follower growth, engagement rate, click-through rate, and conversions may be measured using social media analytics software.

Achievable:

Based on your present skills, resources, and industry standards, set reasonable and doable objectives. Setting unreasonable expectations might result in disappointment and demotivation, even while bold aims can inspire. Determine what is feasible for your company by examining industry trends and your historical performance.

Relevant:

Make sure your social media objectives complement your marketing plan and company goals. In order to be sure that your social media activities are helping your company succeed, it is helpful to set relevant objectives. For instance, increasing sales is your main goal as a firm. Then, your social media objective can be to use your channels to generate a certain amount of leads or conversions.

Time-bound:

Set a deadline or duration for yourself to meet your social media objectives. This facilitates work prioritization, attention maintenance, and progress monitoring over time. Additionally, deadlines may create a feeling of urgency in your team, encouraging them to work diligently toward the objectives.

Your social media marketing campaign will have a clear roadmap if you define SMART objectives. This will make it easier for you to spend resources wisely, track your progress, and modify your plan as needed to guarantee success.

3. Select the Social Media Sites That Are Best for Your Company

hands displaying signs with the logos of social media sites, including Facebook, Instagram, Snapchat, YouTube, and TikTok. To choose the most effective social media platforms for marketing, you must first get knowledge about your target market's tastes and online habits. It's critical to ascertain the websites and content types that your prospective clients frequent most often.

Next, think about the industry, specialty, and marketing goals for your business. Different platforms have different user demographics and provide different possibilities. For example, Instagram is better suited for visual storytelling and reaching younger audiences, whereas LinkedIn is better for professional networking and B2B marketing.

The following are some social networking sites to think about (and why):

Instagram: Well-liked by younger audiences due to its visual appeal, Instagram is perfect for sharing pictures, videos, and Stories. Brands may interact with their audience by using tools like IGTV, Reels, and Instagram Shopping.

YouTube: Being the biggest platform for sharing videos, YouTube enables companies to produce and distribute instructional videos, product reviews, and other types of video content. Companies may utilize YouTube advertisements to reach their target audience and grow their subscriber base.

Facebook: As the biggest social media network, Facebook has over 2.8 billion monthly active users, making it a top option for companies trying to reach a broad audience. For marketing objectives, it provides tools like Facebook Pages, Groups, Ads, and Messenger.

Twitter (X): Twitter is a quick-witted social media site that emphasizes current events and popular subjects. It works well for tweeting, retweeting, and using hashtags to interact with customers while disseminating news, updates, and customer service.

TikTok: With an emphasis on brief, imaginative films, TikTok has grown in popularity, especially among Gen Z users. To connect with this younger demographic, brands may conduct

TikTok ad campaigns, work with influencers, or take advantage of the platform's organic reach.

Pinterest: Pinterest is an online visual discovery tool that lets users look for and save "pins" images that are relevant to their interests. Because it can send websites high-quality referral traffic, it's perfect for companies in the fashion, home décor, cuisine, and do-it-yourself sectors.

LinkedIn: B2B marketing, job hunting, and industry networking are the main uses of this professional networking site. To attract a professional audience, businesses may conduct focused ad campaigns, provide updates, and establish LinkedIn profiles.

Examine the social media presence of your rivals to find out which platforms they use and how effective their tactics are there. This may provide you with insights on what works and what doesn't, as well as assist you in identifying the platforms that are most successful for your sector.

Lastly, think about your abilities and resources for successfully managing many social media profiles. Spreading your efforts too thin and doing poorly across many channels is preferable than concentrating on and becoming excellent at a few platforms.

4. Disseminate Storytelling Content

In order to effectively tell tales on social media, you must develop engrossing, relevant, and shareable narratives that connect with your audience. By knowing your target audience and what interests them, you can create tales that inspire, educate, and amuse. The following techniques may help you use social media material to successfully communicate stories:

Pay attention to the human factor:

People connect with one another, not impersonal companies. Share personal anecdotes about your consumers, employees, and local community to show off the human aspect of your company. Present your company's culture, acknowledge staff accomplishments, or share client success stories to establish a more approachable and human brand image.

Include narrative strategies:

Make use of tried-and-true narrative strategies including scene establishing, character introduction, conflict development, and resolution. These components support the development of a narrative arc that draws readers in and keeps them interested in the plot.

Place a strong emphasis on emotions by creating material that inspires joy, empathy, belonging, or other positive feelings. By strengthening the connection between your brand and your audience, emotional tales may boost sharing, engagement, and loyalty.

Utilize images to improve your narratives:

Visual components like pictures, movies, and graphics may improve the effectiveness and memorability of your narrative. Utilize the impact of visual storytelling by producing visually striking images, infographics, or little films to go along with your message.

Make advantage of material created by users:

Invite people in your audience to narrate their experiences with your company or merchandise. User-generated material enhances its credibility and appeal by bringing relatability, authenticity, and social proof.

Produce material in instalments:

Divide your narrative into manageable, recurring segments that may be distributed gradually. This strategy may assist create a sense of anticipation and motivate your readers to keep reading the story.

Grab the attention of your audience:

Promote communication and input by posing queries, soliciting remarks, or holding surveys. By doing this, you may increase audience engagement and learn more about their preferences, all of which can help you improve your storytelling technique.

Maintain authenticity and relevance:

Make sure your tales are in line with the message and values of your business, and concentrate on subjects that your audience finds interesting and relatable. In order to tell tales that captivate and resonate with your social media audience, authenticity and relevance are essential.

You may tell tales with engaging content created just for your social media audience by using these tactics. This will increase engagement, help you forge closer bonds with your followers, and ultimately improve the outcomes of your social media marketing campaigns.

5. Using Influencer Marketing to Increase Your Audience

For companies trying to reach a wider audience on social media, influencer marketing may be an effective strategy. Businesses may use influencers' authenticity and credibility to market their goods and services by collaborating with them if they have a strong online following and engaged audience.

To properly use influencer marketing, businesses should choose influencers that share the same values as their target audience and brand. These influencers must to be well-known, genuinely connected to their audience, and provide material that enhances the company's offerings.

Once the right influencers have been found, companies may form profitable alliances. This might include joint content development, product reviews, freebies, and sponsored pieces. The nature of the partnership should be determined by the influencer's target audience's preferences as well as the company's unique marketing goals.

Influencer collaborations may also be utilized to jointly produce interesting and genuine content that highlights the brand. Influencers may be invited by companies to take part in live events, interviews, or behind-the-scenes material that will be posted on both the influencer's and the company's social media pages. By humanizing the brand, this material may increase its relatability and appeal to prospective buyers.

To guarantee a return on investment, influencer marketing efforts must be closely monitored. Metrics like engagement, reach, and conversions are important for businesses to monitor in order to assess the success of a collaboration and make the required modifications. Influencer marketing may be strategically used by businesses to increase their social media presence, gain the confidence of prospective clients, and spur development.

6. Make Use of Live Streaming, Pictures, and Videos

By drawing in viewers, encouraging interaction, and raising brand awareness, the use of photos, videos, and live streaming may greatly improve social media marketing. Here's how companies may use these various content kinds to strengthen their social media marketing campaigns:

pictures: Produce aesthetically pleasing, superior pictures that speak to your target market and reflect your brand. These consist of user-generated material, infographics, quotation graphics, and product images. Make sure the colors, styles, and tones of your photos align with the identity of your company. Visuals may improve shareability, spark interest, and break up text-heavy material.

movies: Create brief, interesting movies to introduce your goods, tell a tale, or impart important knowledge. Videos may be utilized for client testimonials, product demonstrations, training, and behind-the-scenes looks at your company. Make sure your movies are mobile-friendly and think about adding subtitles to reach a larger audience. Videos may help personalize your business and have greater engagement rates than static photos.

Real-time streaming: Use live streaming services to interact with your audience in real time, such as Facebook Live, Instagram Live, or LinkedIn Live. For industry events, Q&A sessions, product debuts, and interviews, use live streaming. A unique chance to engage with your audience, respond to their queries, and get quick response is provided via live broadcasting. This promotes brand loyalty and a feeling of community.

Try alternative content forms, including as Reels, Instagram Stories, YouTube Shorts, and TikTok videos, to adjust to the tastes of your audience and maintain the relevance of your material. These formats work effectively for drawing in users with short attention spans because they facilitate rapid, imaginative storytelling.

Adapt your visual material to the particular characteristics and user habits of each social media network. For Twitter, utilize attention-grabbing headlines and images, or make vertical videos for Instagram Stories.

Encourage people who are interested in your business or goods to contribute their photos, videos, or live streams with you. The use of user-generated content into your marketing campaigns enhances their attractiveness to prospective clients by providing social proof, relatability, and authenticity.

You may produce interesting material that draws in viewers, encourages interaction, and eventually boosts brand awareness and client loyalty by combining photos, videos, and live streaming into your social media marketing approach.

7. Increase Your Audience Through Paid Social Media Promotion

Facebook, Instagram, LinkedIn, and Twitter are sites for paid social media advertising.

Advertising on social media entails knowing the particulars of each site, developing engaging and targeted campaigns, and constantly refining your approach to attain better results. When learning how to effectively use sponsored social media advertising, keep the following points in mind:

Start by becoming acquainted with the advertising choices offered by each social media network. Numerous advertising formats, targeting choices, and bidding tactics are available on social media platforms such as Facebook, Instagram, Twitter, LinkedIn, and Pinterest. Having a thorough understanding of the subtle differences between each platform will enable you to allocate your advertising spend wisely.

Next, make sure your advertising strategies have well-defined goals. Your objectives can be to raise sales, generate prospects, increase website traffic, or raise brand recognition. Establishing specific goals can assist you in selecting the best ad formats, targeting choices, and performance indicators to monitor.

When it comes to ad creatives, create eye-catching images and language that captivate viewers and clearly convey your message. To gain the attention of your audience, use attention-grabbing headlines, videos, and high-quality photos. For a consistent user experience, make sure the creatives for your advertisements complement your entire brand identity and message.

One essential component of paid social media advertising is targeting. To reach your desired audience, make use of the platforms' interest-based, behavioral, and demographic targeting tools. To reach individuals who have already engaged with your business or who have traits in common with your current consumers, employ lookalike audiences, custom audiences, or remarketing tools.

Make sure your bid strategy and budget are in line with your goals and intended return on investment. To determine the best method for achieving your campaign objectives, test out various bidding tactics, such as cost per click (CPC), cost per impression (CPM), or cost per action (CPA).

Regularly track and evaluate the results of your advertising activities. Monitor important performance indicators including cost per conversion, return on ad spend (ROAS), and click-through rate (CTR). Utilize these information to improve your targeting, bidding, and ad creative tactics, which will eventually increase the effectiveness of your campaigns as a whole.

Lastly, when it comes to paid social media advertising, use a test-and-learn strategy. Try out various ad styles, targeting choices, and message on a regular basis to see what works best for your audience and business. You may maximize your return on investment and optimize your campaigns with the aid of this iterative method.

You can master paid social media advertising and get the most out of your investment in this potent marketing channel by concentrating on these factors.

8. Increase Interest and Develop

Love bubbles and Facebook likes floating up from a phone screen are visual representations of social media activity provided by Community via Conversations.

In order to increase social media engagement and create a devoted following around your business, dialogue is essential. You may build a real relationship with your audience, show off the personality of your company, and get insightful feedback from your followers by having meaningful discussions with them.

Engaging in dialogue on social media allows you to humanize your brand by demonstrating that actual people are running the company and are interested in the thoughts and worries of their followers. This fosters honesty and trust, which increases the relatability and approachability of your brand.

By encouraging visitors to participate with your material, conversations also increase user engagement. You provide your audience with chances to interact with your brand by posing queries, soliciting remarks, and so on. Because social media algorithms reward material with high involvement, this increased engagement results in improved exposure on those sites.

It takes constant work and a customer-focused mindset to create a community via dialogue. You can show that your audience matters by really hearing what they have to say and taking the time to answer any issues they may have. Increased client happiness, loyalty, and advocacy may result from this.

Speaking with your audience also gives you important insights into their requirements, preferences, and problem issues. You may utilize these data to improve your entire customer experience, product offers, and social media strategy.

Talks also let you find and establish connections with local influencers and brand evangelists. By fostering these connections, you may increase the reach and legitimacy of your brand by taking advantage of their influence.

In conclusion, social media discussions increase interaction and are essential to creating a devoted, strong community around your business. You can build a more engaged and connected community that supports the long-term success of your business by actively engaging in discussions, showing genuine interest in your audience's thoughts, and encouraging a feeling of belonging.

9. The Function of Contests and User-Generated Content

Your social media marketing campaigns may be greatly enhanced by user-generated content (UGC) and competitions, which promote community, increase engagement, and establish brand trust. Here are some tips for using competitions and user-generated content (UGC) in your social media marketing:

Photo competitions: Inspire people to share images of your goods or services, and provide rewards for the top submissions. This might provide new material for your social media platforms and develop interest around your company.

Campaigns employing hashtags: Come up with a distinctive hashtag for your company and ask others to use it while sharing photos, videos, or experiences. This may raise awareness of your business and motivate more users to interact with your material.

Contests based on testimonials: Invite clients to contribute their achievements or satisfying experiences using your goods or services. Give prizes to the most imaginative or inspirational submissions, and post them on your social media pages to establish your authority.

Video challenges: Ask users to make quick films that highlight their originality, expertise, or brand-related experiences. To promote participation, share the top entries on your social media platforms and provide prizes.

Caption contests: Post a picture or a video, then request clever or catchy caption ideas from your audience. Give out prizes for the best captions, then post them on social media.

Interactive surveys and quizzes about your business or sector are a great way to interact with your audience. This can increase engagement and provide you with insightful information about the tastes and viewpoints of your audience.

Collaborative storytelling: Invite users to contribute their own tales of encounters with your company, then weave them together to create a longer story or series. This can improve the sense of community and your audience's emotional ties.

You may produce more interesting and varied content that connects with your audience, establishes your authority, and grows your online community by implementing user-generated content and competitions into your social media marketing plan.

10. Make use of trends, keywords, and hashtags

Effective use of hashtags, keywords, and trends in your social media marketing can help you become more visible, connect with more people, and maintain relevance in your field. You can use these tools in your social media strategy in the following ways:

Hashtags: On social media sites like LinkedIn, Instagram, and Twitter, hashtags are an effective tool for classifying and organizing content. By utilizing trending and pertinent hashtags, you can expand the audience interested in your niche and improve the discoverability of your content. For maximum exposure, look up industry-specific hashtags and combine branded, popular, and niche hashtags. Steer clear of excessive or pointless hashtag usage, as this may come across as spammy.

Keywords: Incorporating relevant keywords into your social media material helps boost its exposure in search results on social media platforms and search engines. Identify keywords related to your business, brand, and target audience, and weave them organically throughout your material, including captions, descriptions, and biographies. Use keyword research tools to uncover trending and high-volume keywords that may enhance your content's exposure.

Trends: Staying up-to-date with current trends in your sector and popular culture will help you develop timely and relevant content that connects with your audience. Monitor popular topics, news items, and social media discussions to find trends you can use into your social media marketing. Participate in popular topics by using suitable hashtags, giving your thoughts, or generating material that resonates with the trend. This may assist enhance your brand's exposure and establish you as an industry authority.

User-generated content: Encourage your followers to use branded hashtags when they contribute material relating to your goods or services. This will allow you to monitor user-generated material, communicate with your audience, and highlight their experiences with your business.

Analytics: Regularly monitor your social media performance to understand which hashtags, topics, and trends connect with your audience. Use information from your analytics to enhance your content strategy, concentrating on what works best for your brand and audience.

Effectively employing hashtags, keywords, and trends in your social media marketing, you can boost your content's exposure, remain current in your business, and generate compelling material that connects with your target audience.

11. Analyze Social Media and Modify Your Approach

Measuring social media analytics is vital for determining the efficiency of your marketing efforts and making educated choices to change your approach. Here's how you can monitor data and adapt your plan accordingly:

Set specific objectives: Define your social media goals, such as improving brand recognition, driving website traffic, generating leads, or boosting sales. Setting clear goals can assist you in selecting the appropriate metrics to monitor and assess your progress.

Determine the KPIs, or key performance indicators: Determine which KPIs are most relevant to your objectives in light of your aims. Click-through rate (CTR), conversion rate, reach, impressions, engagement metrics (likes, comments, shares), and return on investment (ROI) are examples of common KPIs.

Employ analytics tools: Make use of the built-in resources offered by social media sites, such as LinkedIn Analytics, Facebook Insights,

Twitter Analytics, and Instagram Insights. Furthermore, take into account using other resources such as Hootsuite, Sprout Social, or Google Analytics in order to compile more comprehensive information and assess platform effectiveness.

Regularly analyze data: Keep an eye on your social media statistics to follow your progress over time. Seek for any trends, patterns, or oddities that can point to areas for development or success. This will assist you in modifying your approach using data-driven judgments.

Modify your approach to content: Determine which content kinds, when to publish them, and in what forms work best for your audience based on your statistics. To further engage your audience, iterate your content strategy by concentrating on what already works well and trying with new concepts.

Optimize targeting and ad expenditure: If you're doing sponsored social media efforts, make the most of your targeting and ad spending by using analytics data. To optimize your return on investment, experiment with various bidding tactics and adjust your targeting choices to reach the correct audience.

Try and discover: Test several facets of your social media marketing on a regular basis, including posting schedules, content kinds, and interaction strategies. Analyze your audience and brand to find out what resonates with them the most, then use this information to inform your approach.

Review and iterate: Evaluate your social media performance on a regular basis and tweak your plan as needed. This might include revising your techniques, KPIs, or objectives to better reflect your aims and target audience's preferences.

You can maximize your marketing efforts, get better results, and guarantee a higher return on investment for your social media campaigns by monitoring social media analytics and modifying your plan based on data-driven insights.

12. Plan and Schedule Your Content for Social Media

Time may be saved, productivity can be raised, and consistency in posting can be ensured by automating and scheduling social media marketing material. Take these actions to plan and automate your social media content:

Make a content calendar: Plan out the times that you will publish on the various social media networks. This will assist you with content planning, consistency, and posting a variety of content kinds, including informative, entertaining, and promotional pieces.

Make use of social media management tools: Make use of social media management tools to plan and automate content on many channels. Sprout Social, Later, Hootsuite, and Buffer are a few of the well-liked tools. You may schedule posts for publishing dates and times, add captions and hashtags, and upload material using these tools.

Batch content development: Prepare many articles at once and set up certain time periods for content creation rather than writing material every day. Long-term time savings and the maintenance of a regular posting schedule are both facilitated by this.

Repurpose content: Make it into a new piece of writing for a new platform or format to get the most out of it. Consider transforming a blog article into an infographic, a movie, or a string of postings on social media. By doing this, you'll be able to keep up a regular content schedule without having to invest additional time in content creation.

Engage automatically: Social media management solutions keep an eye on messages, comments, and mentions on several sites. To save time and keep your audience engaged consistently, set up automatic answers for frequently asked queries or comments.

Evaluate performance: Continually assess your social media performance to determine the optimal posting times, the kinds of material that connect with your audience, and the best strategies for interaction. Make adjustments to your posting schedule and content calendar based on these findings.

Establish content curation: In order to enhance your unique content, think about selecting relevant news pieces, publications, and other materials from influential people in the sector. Make use of content curation tools such as Scoop, Pocket, and Feedly.it to find and arrange material that fits the interests of your audience and your business. To keep a well-balanced content mix, schedule well chosen material in addition to your own postings.

You may boost productivity, keep a regular posting schedule, and free up time to concentrate on other elements of your marketing plan by automating and scheduling your social media marketing material.

13. Appreciate Input and Guard Your Online Image

visible input from social media represented by floating bubbles with ratings and reviews from phones
Managing the online reputation of your business requires responding to criticism on social media. It's critical to respond to unfavorable remarks or critiques with professionalism, sensitivity, and promptness.

First, keep a careful eye out for any unfavorable comments on your social media accounts. Reacting promptly shows that your company values its clients and is aware of their issues. In some cases, prompt action may even stop a bad situation from becoming worse.

Always react to bad comments with grace, decency, and empathy. Recognize the customer's sentiments and demonstrate that you comprehend their problems. If needed, express your regret and let them know you value their opinions. Refrain from being combative or defensive as this might further harm the image of your company.

Before answering, take some time to look into the matter so that you can provide precise details and a concise solution. Inform the client that you are investigating the complicated problem and will get back to them as soon as feasible with a solution.

In your answer, if a resolution is feasible, provide it to the client. This can come in the form of a reimbursement, a substitution, or a free service. In addition to demonstrating your dedication to client satisfaction, you may be able to turn a bad experience around by confronting the problem head-on and offering a solution.

Asking the client to get in touch with you privately by phone, email, or direct message may be suitable in some situations to move the topic offline. This makes it possible to take a more tailored approach and may stop the problem from becoming worse in a public setting.

It's also crucial to take criticism to heart and use it into insights for bettering your goods, services, or social media marketing initiatives. Examine the comments to find any trends or reoccurring problems that may need to be fixed in your company's operations.

Lastly, keep up a strong online presence by regularly posting insightful information and interacting with your followers. This can assist you in developing a favorable reputation and brand image, which might lessen the effect of sporadic unfavorable comments.

14. Make sure your whole marketing plan incorporates your social media marketing strategy.

By combining your social media and offline marketing techniques, you can expand the reach of both and provide a consistent brand experience. The following are some strategies for combining your physical and internet marketing efforts:

Promote social media accounts: Put your hashtags and social media handles on printed marketing materials including brochures, flyers, business cards, banners, and packaging. In order to keep informed about your most recent news and products, this encourages your offline audience to engage with you online.

Use QR codes: Print materials, event signs, and in-store displays may all benefit from the inclusion of QR codes. When scanned, these codes route people to your website, social media accounts, or targeted online campaigns. Your offline audience may interact with your digital presence more easily as a result.

In-store marketing: Use in-store marketing to get consumers to interact with your content or follow your social media profiles. Give consumers who check in, write a review, or post a picture of their purchase on social media with a branded hashtag a discount or exclusive offer, for instance.

Utilize events: At offline gatherings like conferences, trade exhibits, or seminars, advertise your social media presence. Encourage participants to tweet, post, or communicate with them in real time by using the event hashtag to share their experiences.

Use user-generated content: Incorporate user-generated content from your social media platforms into print advertisements, in-store displays, and even digital screens at events as part of your offline marketing collateral. This promotes greater online brand interaction from consumers and aids in the development of social proof.

Cross-promote campaigns: Make complementary social media content for an offline marketing campaign you're running. On the other hand, use your social media platforms to advertise offline events or campaigns so that consumers are aware of your marketing initiatives from both online and offline.

Work together with influencers: Assist local influencers that have a sizable online and offline following. To generate excitement both online and offline, use their influence for offline events like meet-and-greets and product launches.

Maintain a consistent brand across all offline and online marketing materials by making sure your business's visual identity, message, and tone are the same. This facilitates the development of a cohesive brand experience, which makes it simpler for clients to identify and interact with your business.

You may expand your audience, provide a consistent brand experience, and increase the effectiveness of both offline and social media marketing initiatives by combining them.

As this chapter has shown, optimizing your social media marketing approach requires a blend of approaches, ranging from establishing SMART objectives and producing captivating content to using influencers and merging digital and traditional marketing initiatives. By using these techniques, you may successfully draw in your audience's interest, pique their curiosity about your business, and motivate them to act.

9 7 9 8 8 7 2 1 0 4 8 1 0